PHILADELPHIA
EAGLES

BY WILL GRAVES

SportsZone

An Imprint of Abdo Publishing
abdopublishing.com

abdopublishing.com

Published by Abdo Publishing, a division of ABDO, PO Box 398166, Minneapolis, Minnesota 55439. Copyright © 2017 by Abdo Consulting Group, Inc. International copyrights reserved in all countries. No part of this book may be reproduced in any form without written permission from the publisher. SportsZone™ is a trademark and logo of Abdo Publishing.

Printed in the United States of America, North Mankato, Minnesota
042016
092016

Cover Photo: Matt Rourke/AP Images
Interior Photos: Matt Rourke/AP Images, 1; G. Paul Burnett/AP Images, 4-5; Bill Kostroun/AP Images, 6-7; Bettmann/Corbis, 8-9, 12; Pro Football Hall of Fame/AP Images, 10, 11, 13; Pro Football Hall of Fame/AP Images, 11; AP Images, 14-15; Clem Murray/AP Images, 16-17; Paul Spinelli/AP Images, 18-19; Kevin Terrell/AP Images, 20; Damian Strohmeyer/AP Images, 21; Paul Sancya/AP Images, 22-23; Jeff Roberson/AP Images, 24; G. Newman Lowrance/AP Images, 25; Scott Boehm/AP Images, 26-27; John Bazemore/AP Images, 28-29

Editor: Patrick Donnelly
Series Designer: Nikki Farinella

Cataloging-in-Publication Data
Names: Graves, Will, author.
Title: Philadelphia Eagles / by Will Graves.
Description: Minneapolis, MN : Abdo Publishing, [2017] | Series: NFL up close | Includes index.
Identifiers: LCCN 2015960449 | ISBN 9781680782295 (lib. bdg.) | ISBN 9781680776409 (ebook)
Subjects: LCSH: Philadelphia Eagles (Football team)--History--Juvenile literature. | National Football League--Juvenile literature. | Football--Juvenile literature. | Professional sports--Juvenile literature. | Football teams--Pennsylvania--Juvenile literature.
Classification: DDC 796.332--dc23
LC record available at http://lccn.loc.gov/2015960449

TABLE OF CONTENTS

Herman Edwards pounces on the Giants' ill-timed fumble in 1978.

A LUCKY BREAK

Things looked bad for the Philadelphia Eagles in their 1978 game at Giants Stadium in the New Jersey Meadowlands. The New York Giants led 17-12 and had the ball with 31 seconds to play. All they had to do was take a knee, and they would send the Eagles back to Philadelphia with a loss.

But the Eagles caught a lucky break. Instead of taking a knee, New York quarterback Joe Pisarcik tried to give the ball to fullback Larry Csonka. They fumbled the handoff. Philadelphia defensive back Herman Edwards scooped it up. When he looked up, there were no Giants in front of him.

Edwards raced to the end zone for a 26-yard touchdown. The New York fans screamed in shock. The Eagles won 19-17 in one of the most famous finishes in National Football League (NFL) history. The play became known as "The Miracle at the Meadowlands."

Philadelphia took advantage of its good fortune. The Eagles finished 1978 with a 9-7 record and made the playoffs for the first time since 1960.

In 2010, the Eagles did it to the Giants again. DeSean Jackson returned a punt for a touchdown on the last play to beat the Giants at their new stadium.

DeSean Jackson races to the end zone on a last-second punt return to shock the Giants in 2010.

FLY, EAGLES, FLY

The Philadelphia Eagles were founded in 1933. They had a rough start. They lost their first NFL game 56-0 to the New York Giants. There were a lot of games like that during the Eagles' first decade. They finished with a losing record in each of their first 10 seasons.

That changed in the 1940s, thanks to Hall of Fame running back Steve Van Buren. With Van Buren bulling his way through opposing defenses, the Eagles soared. Philadelphia lost the NFL title game in 1947 but then won it in 1948 and 1949.

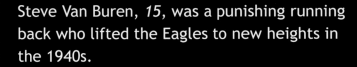
Steve Van Buren, *15*, was a punishing running back who lifted the Eagles to new heights in the 1940s.

FAST FACT

Steve Van Buren was called "Wham Bam" because of the way he would run over defenders. He was the NFL's all-time leading rusher with 5,860 yards when he retired in 1951.

Van Buren scored the only touchdown in the 1948 championship game. He plowed through the Chicago Cardinals and the blizzard-like conditions at Philadelphia's Shibe Park for a 7-0 Eagles victory. But Van Buren almost missed the game. He saw the snow that morning and thought the game would be postponed. He did not head to the stadium until coach Greasy Neale called to tell him they were still going to play.

A year later, Van Buren rushed for 196 yards as the Eagles topped the Los Angeles Rams 14-0 for a second straight title.

Steve Van Buren plows through the snow to score the only touchdown of the 1948 NFL Championship Game.

10

Steve Van Buren and coach Earle "Greasy" Neale are surrounded by happy Eagles players after they beat the Cardinals.

FAST FACT

Bert Bell helped found the Eagles and served as their coach from 1936 to 1940. He later went to work as the NFL commissioner from 1946 to 1959.

11

REVIVAL

The Eagles did not make the playoffs in the 1950s.
But they won their third NFL championship in 1960.
Quarterback Norm Van Brocklin and tough guy Chuck
Bednarik were the stars. Bednarik was the last of the
great two-way players in the NFL. He was the Eagles'
starting center on offense and a starting linebacker on
defense. Van Brocklin won the NFL Most Valuable Player
(MVP) award that year.

Norm Van Brocklin throws a pass against
the Green Bay Packers in the 1960 NFL
Championship Game.

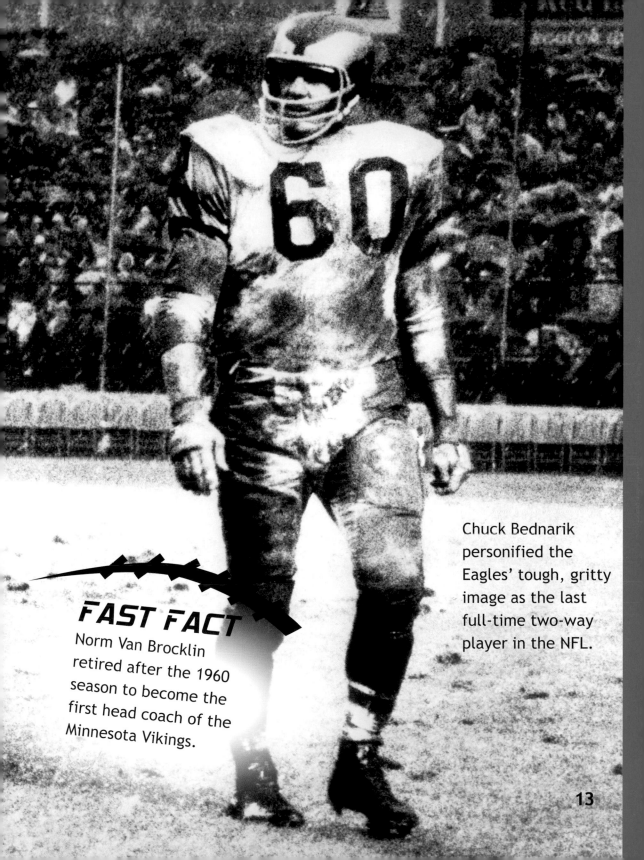

FAST FACT

Norm Van Brocklin retired after the 1960 season to become the first head coach of the Minnesota Vikings.

Chuck Bednarik personified the Eagles' tough, gritty image as the last full-time two-way player in the NFL.

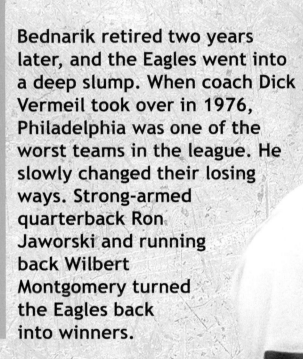

Bednarik retired two years later, and the Eagles went into a deep slump. When coach Dick Vermeil took over in 1976, Philadelphia was one of the worst teams in the league. He slowly changed their losing ways. Strong-armed quarterback Ron Jaworski and running back Wilbert Montgomery turned the Eagles back into winners.

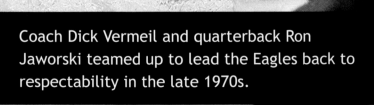

Coach Dick Vermeil and quarterback Ron Jaworski teamed up to lead the Eagles back to respectability in the late 1970s.

15

The Eagles made the playoffs four straight years between 1978 and 1981. In 1980, they knocked off their division rival, the Dallas Cowboys, to make it to their first Super Bowl. However, they came up short. Jaworski threw three interceptions in a 27-10 loss to the Oakland Raiders.

Wilbert Montgomery scampers into the end zone in a playoff game against the Minnesota Vikings on January 3, 1981.

Randall Cunningham was one of the most exciting dual-threat quarterbacks in NFL history.

18

BUDDY BALL

Buddy Ryan took over as coach of the Eagles in 1986. Ryan and Philadelphia were made for each other. He fit right in with the city's brash image. Ryan talked a big game, and his defenses played one, too. He built one of the most feared defenses the NFL has ever seen.

The Eagles called it "Buddy Ball." In Buddy Ball, the defense was free to attack the quarterback. Led by star defensive linemen Reggie White and Jerome Brown, Philadelphia made the playoffs three straight years from 1988 to 1990.

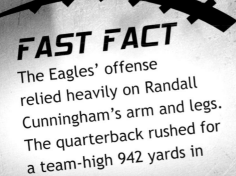

FAST FACT

The Eagles' offense relied heavily on Randall Cunningham's arm and legs. The quarterback rushed for a team-high 942 yards in 1990 alone.

Sometimes Buddy Ball would get the coach in trouble because of how rough the Eagles played. Ryan seemed to enjoy riling up opponents. While Ryan's time with Philadelphia was successful, controversy seemed to follow him. The team's owners grew tired of seeing the coach's name in the headlines. And Ryan's Eagles went 0-3 in playoff games. He was fired after the 1990 season.

FAST FACT

The Eagles-Bears 1988 playoff game at Chicago's Soldier Field became known as the "Fog Bowl." A thick fog made it tough to see the field. The Bears won 20-12.

Visibility was severely limited when the Eagles faced the Bears in the "Fog Bowl" game.

Reggie White was the anchor of the great
Philadelphia defense of the late 1980s.

MAGNIFICENT McNABB

Philadelphia is called the "City of Brotherly Love." But there was not much love to go around at the 1999 NFL Draft. The Eagles selected quarterback Donovan McNabb with the second overall pick. Their fans wanted the Eagles to take running back Ricky Williams instead. And they let their displeasure be known—loudly.

McNabb worked hard to change the boos into cheers. He could dazzle defenders with his quick feet or beat them with one of the strongest arms in the NFL. By his second season, the Eagles were back in the playoffs.

Donovan McNabb became the focus of the Philadelphia offense when the Eagles drafted him in 1999.

That was the start of a five-year run in which Philadelphia was one of the best teams in football. Under coach Andy Reid the Eagles won at least 11 games per season between 2000 and 2004. They also won four division titles over that stretch.

Philadelphia was not quite so fantastic in the playoffs, though. The Eagles lost in the conference championship game in three straight years. They finally made it to the Super Bowl after the 2004 season. McNabb threw three touchdown passes, but the New England Patriots held on to win 24-21.

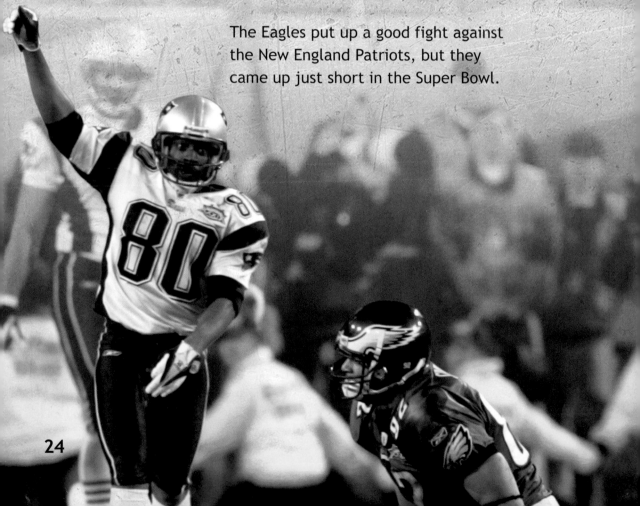

The Eagles put up a good fight against the New England Patriots, but they came up just short in the Super Bowl.

Andy Reid oversaw one of the most successful eras of Eagles football.

FAST FACT

Andy Reid enjoyed unmatched success during his 14 years coaching the Eagles. He posted a record of 130–93–1 before leaving after the 2012 season.

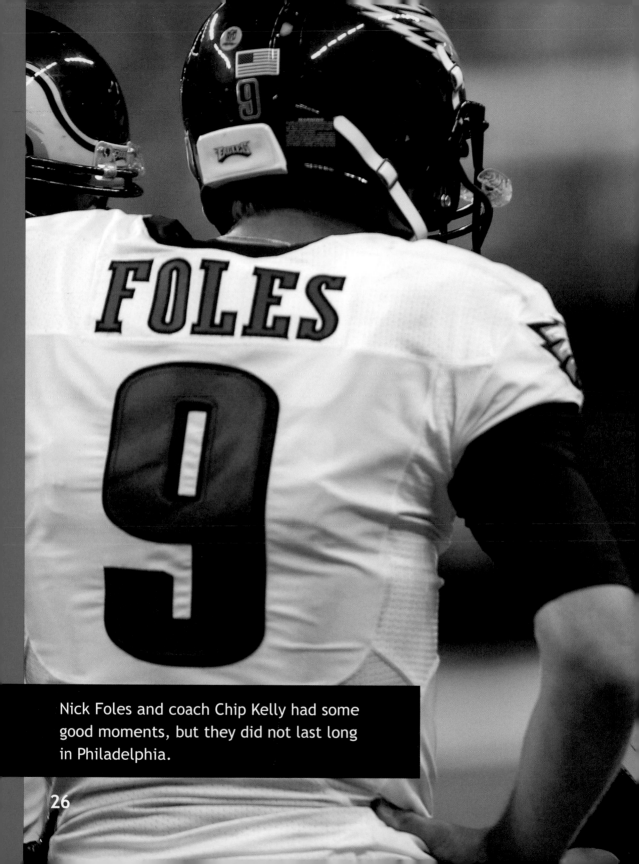

Nick Foles and coach Chip Kelly had some good moments, but they did not last long in Philadelphia.

CHIP AND A CHANGE

The Eagles were looking for a change after Andy Reid left. They found it in Chip Kelly. Kelly had never coached in the NFL when Philadelphia hired him in 2013. Kelly made a name for himself as a college coach with the high-scoring Oregon Ducks.

Kelly wasted little time making a difference. In 2013, the Eagles went 10-6 in his first season, a six-win improvement over 2012. Philadelphia finished fourth in the league in scoring. Quarterback Nick Foles tied an NFL record with seven touchdown passes in a victory over the Oakland Raiders. The Eagles won their division in 2013 and went 10-6 in 2014.

But in 2014 the Eagles
traded Foles to the Rams for
quarterback Sam Bradford.
And after a disastrous 2015
season, Philadelphia made
another coaching change. The
Eagles fired Kelly and hired
Doug Pederson to guide the
team into the future. Pederson
is a former Eagles quarterback
and previously helped lead the
Kansas City Chiefs' offense.
Philadelphia fans hope he can
work with Bradford and running
back DeMarco Murray to turn
the Eagles into an offensive
powerhouse again.

Sam Bradford fires
a pass against the
Atlanta Falcons
in 2015.

FAST FACT

Running back LeSean McCoy set a team record with 1,607 rushing yards while being named an All-Pro in 2013.

TIMELINE

1933

The Philadelphia Eagles begin play, finishing their first season with a 3-5-1 record.

1943

Due to player shortages during World War II, the Eagles combine with the Pittsburgh Steelers for one season. The "Steagles" go 5-4-1 and finish third in their division.

1948

The Eagles beat the Chicago Cardinals in a snowstorm 7-0 for their first championship.

1960

Ted Dean's 5-yard touchdown in the fourth quarter lifts the Eagles past the Green Bay Packers 17-13 to win the club's third NFL title.

1981

On January 11, the Philadelphia defense limits the Dallas Cowboys to 206 total yards in a 20-7 victory to send the Eagles to their first Super Bowl.

1999

Philadelphia selects quarterback Donovan McNabb with the second overall pick in the NFL Draft. McNabb goes on to make six Pro Bowls with the Eagles.

2005

The Eagles pull away in the second half for a 27-10 win over Atlanta on January 23, clinching a berth in the Super Bowl.

2016

Doug Pederson is hired to replace Chip Kelly as the Eagles' head coach.

GLOSSARY

CONTROVERSY
Unwanted negative attention.

DRAFT
The process by which leagues determine which teams can sign new players coming into the league.

FUMBLE
When a player with the ball loses possession, allowing the opponent a chance to recover it.

PLAYOFFS
A set of games after the regular season that decides which team will be the champion.

ROOKIE
A first-year player.

SACK
A tackle of the quarterback behind the line of scrimmage before he can pass the ball.

SLUMP
A period of time when a player or team is not doing well.

TWO-WAY PLAYER
A player who plays both offense and defense, a common practice from the early days of the NFL through the 1950s.

INDEX

ABOUT THE AUTHOR

Will Graves grew up in Maryland fearing the Philadelphia Eagles while cheering for the Washington Redskins. He has spent more than 20 years as a sportswriter and is the author of more than a dozen books. He lives in Pittsburgh, where he covers the NFL, the NHL, and Major League Baseball for the Associated Press.